C000231742

MONDEO MAN

Luke Wright is a poet and broadcaster. His poetry stage shows have toured the world and played sold-out runs in London and Edinburgh. He is a regular contributor to BBC Radio and his verse documentary on Channel 4 was nominated for a Grierson Award. *Mondeo Man* is his first full collection.

ALSO BY LUKE WRIGHT

The Vile Ascent Of Lucien Gore And What The People Did
(Nasty Little Press, 2011)
High Performance (Nasty Little Press, 2009)

Mondeo Man

Luke Wright

Penned in the Margins

LONDON

PUBLISHED BY PENNED IN THE MARGINS
Toynbee Studios, 28 Commercial Street, London E1 6AB
www.pennedinthemargins.co.uk

First published 2013

Printed in the United Kingdom by Bell & Bain Ltd.

ISBN
978-1-908058-09-6

CONTENTS

ACKNOWLEDGEMENTS

The following publications published one or more of the poems in this collection: *The Sunday Times, Magma, Five Dials, Hand+Star, The Spectator* and *The Morning Star.*

'Loughborough', 'Stansted', 'Another Grotty Holiday', 'Luke's Got A Joke' and 'Mondeo Man' were previously published in *High Performance* (Nasty Little Press, 2009).

A version of 'The Ballad of Chris & Ann's Fish Bar' was presented as a radio play on BBC Radio 4's Verse Illustrated in August 2011. 'A Hornchurch Commuter' was commissioned by The Queens Theatre, Hornchurch. 'About a Minute' was featured as part of The Gopher Hole's inaugural exhibition of the same title. 'The Billionaire Princess', 'Last Orders', Thaxted', 'For Radio' and 'Royal Wedding, 1947' were all commissions for BBC Radio 4's Saturday Live.

The author would like to thank: Tom Chivers at Penned in the Margins; Chris Gribble; Tania Harrison; the Aisle16 poets — Tim Clare, Joe Dunthorne, Chris Hicks, John Osborne, Joel Stickley and Ross Sutherland; and his parents John and Annette Wright. Particular thanks are due to Clare Pollard without whom these poems would never have made it off the stage.

The author gratefully acknowledges the receipt of a grant from Arts Council England.

Much love and thanks goes to Sally, Aidan and Sam.

Mondeo Man

for Sally, Aidan & Sam

Mondeo Man

A Hornchurch Commuter

It's Winter and I leave my home in darkness
to schlep down Suttons Gardens, Stations Lane,
then past the rows of houses lost to commerce:
the florist, cabbies, bookies, café, train.

They call this game the rat race but it's not —
these sad and silty mornings pocked with sighs;
there's nothing fast about this way of life —
just deep ruts cut slow into the mind's eye.

I spend my Mondays living for the weekend —
who doesn't here, eh, that's the way it works;
that's why we brought our families to the suburbs
to live on London's green and pleasant skirt.

Inside this fizzing fence of motorway,
our tiny crumbs of Essex neatly mortgaged,
a low-rent Metroland for boys done good;
a place to deckchair doze in heavy August.

And for that right we clatter down these traintracks
through greyish sprawl from Dagenham to Bow
where London's mouth lies waiting. Grin and bear it:
inhale, exhale then underground you go.

The Drunk Train

Pull back the crimson curtain stained
with blood of dramas past,
on city clerks zigzagging home,
their Tie Rack ties half mast;

on London's horns, on suet air,
on gummy pavement slabs,
peroxide Oompa Loompa girls
who dribble their kebabs;

on unforgiving betting shops,
on endless Maccy Dees,
discarded right-wing newspapers,
on boozers slick with sleaze.

Britannia's on the sauce again;
she's drinking hard tonight:
a hip flask at the Cenotaph,
a dance in ginger light.

In panelled clubs on wingback chairs
chaps foster drinks and gout
as Bacchus swipes their credit cards,
and wide boys start to shout

in West End clubs where bass lines throb
and dirty sex bombs tick;
where chat-up lines are slaughtered and
the Red Bull flows like sick;

as gel-skulled lads in Topman checks
and Richard Hammond dreams
trash Allah, drinking Stella,
shouting shit at plasma screens;

till all the tiny insect folk
in Smirnoff Ice elation
escort their mates down Bishopsgate
to Liverpool Street Station.

Now the drunk train pulls through city streets,
a half-cut girly texts and tweets,
a baby-boomer guards his seat.
The air is dead, a fetid heat
begins to build, the carriage hums.
  Soon songs will come,
  soon songs will come,
  soon songs will come,
  soon songs...

At home, divorcees slurp from cans
and curse the years they gave;
they watch their vindaloos congeal
and *Mock The Week* on Dave.

While haggard working mothers stand
on icy kitchen floors
awaiting midnight kettles while
their feckless partners snore;

the young professional couples slob,
their sofas over-sized,
too tired to think or fuck or blink
their oyster-lidded eyes.

They used to be the students playing
Jenga with the bin
but who cares about tomorrow
when the snakebite's kicking in.

The drunk train rolls through sleepy 'burbs;
on board the buzz of slurring words
is heard above the diesel's burr.
The edges of the evening blur.
It all begins to mean something
    and soon they'll sing,
    and soon they'll sing,
    and soon they'll sing,
    and soon...

They'll sing the words to tinny songs
they heard when they were young,
the words they scrawled on folder backs
or shouted at their mums;

the pop songs that were playing when
they kissed their teenage crush,
the empty couplet auto-tuned
until it's sonic mush.

They'll howl with aching arteries
devoid of tune or flair,
repeat the vapid chorus lines
as if they were a prayer.

They'll sing just as their ancestors
would make a fire and chant;
all legless croons and bludgeoned tunes,
they'll sing until they can't.

The drunk train trundles through our towns
that wear a silent eiderdown,
their wick turned up, their volume down,
a thousand snores, a thousand frowns.
But on the train they're singing now,
a fatalistic bloody row
of consonants mistreating vowels
that comes from lungs and mouths and bowels;
no stage nor mic nor interval,
just ballads blunt and cynical,
with Bacchanalian refrains
and all the pith of human pain,
their words of love and sex and strife
excoriating modern life:

they sing tonight,
they sing tonight
they sing tonight,
they sing tonight...

So, gentle folk, you second rowers,
Guardian readers, theatre-goers,
let's sing tonight, let's sing tonight.
Let's peer behind Britannia's grin,
let's shake her towns like money tins,
let's scour the malls and plummy clubs,
collecting folk from dingy pubs
until this tiny bedroom swells
with bullies, cads and ne'er-do-wells;
let's wind them up with iambic
until we see what makes them tick,
let's make them run a maze of words,
of banter crude and scenes absurd:
  let's sing tonight,
  let's sing tonight,
  let's sing tonight,
  let's sing tonight,
  till either them or us has cracked,
  till either them or us has cracked.

Thaxted

To Essex then, the one the kids don't know,
where Tudor shops are soaked in yeasty sun
and summer afternoons are sweet and slow.
It's here the bearded morris dancers come
to shake their bells and hankies, whack their sticks,
oblivious to Thomas Beecham's sneer,
to jig, mum, molly up in bygone kits
and drown the cricket dusk in warm, flat beer.
As suited snakes in London cry "Progressive!"
and rally round the sound of ringing tills,
in Thaxted men in whites and ribbon tresses
dance backwards past the dark satanic mills.
And on, into a creamy, moonlit silence:
religion in a world of certain science.

Get Parochial!

Come, join me in my quaint provincial town.
You have to meet my barber. He collects
memorabilia relating to the War
and will scarcely raise an eyebrow when you say
that *Nicaragua really changed your life*.

Read ye not Haruki Murakami!
Read instead the Norwich Evening News!
Say what? A man from Diss has found a coin –
they say it might be Dutch, now there's a thing.
And look, a 2-4-1 at Wetherspoons.

But please don't bring your friends with Hitler fringes,
the ones whose girlfriends write the *What's Hot* lists,
who spend their weekends *Honking crystal meth*
and use the word 'creative' as a noun.
I'm not sure they'd really like it here.

We'll take the kiddies swimming Sunday morning
with tattooed daddies and their skimpy Britneys
and afterwards indulge in Cup-a-Soups
before a long walk home along the river
to marvel at its narrow span and depth.

Loughborough

I once spent the day with a girl who was pro fox-hunting,
who asked what was wrong with the Tories,
who said she wanted her parents' life.

We lay down outside a church.
The grass poured around us like mint sauce
and I thought maybe I'd just marry her
and be done with it.

Later, we climbed to where the Victorian prison stood,
its windows like diamonds in the low sun,
the skyline beneath us like smashed meringue,
and I thought about the house we'd own
in Loughborough,
our lanky children,
our utility room,
our dogs, wax jackets, fridge calendar and committees.

We sat on our coats, finger-tips touching.
An ice-cream van started like a chesty cough.
The breeze almost gone, the mud almost dry —
it was all just like summer, if you squinted.

Stansted

My Dad used to work for the CAA
in a round building just off High Holborn.

While there he worked on the planning permission
for the control tower at Stansted.

This was the most tangible of his achievements
and whenever Dads were mentioned I'd say:

My Dad was involved with 'The Stansted Project.'
I'd say: *My Dad was like the main boss.*

And on occasion, to proud, freckle-faced boys:
Yeah, well, my Dad ... built Stansted Airport.

And yet, I never really knew what he did.
Not like I knew his mahogany trouser press,

the brass bowl for his change and errant golf tees,
the way his cheek felt cold when he came back from work,

his black Mac' jewelled with rain, smelling of trains
and a faint whiff of the morning's aftershave.

Or the skeleton clocks he spent his weekends making,
meticulous time-keeping under glass domes,

the way he'd rest his hands on his stomach after lunch,
or how his check shirt would show at the neck

of his blue, shabby workshop overalls,
the silver popper at the top undone.

But now, as then, I see him out on a flat field
that is slowly becoming a runway,

clipboard in hand, directing other men,
windsock blowing in the breeze.

Jean-Claude Gendarme

So kiss me quick and crush a can,
the summer's here now make a plan.
Decide on continental sands,
load kiddies, cousins, dogs and Gran
into an ancient caravan
(plus camping gas and tinny pans)
then loudly praise your air con fans,
look forward to the *autobahns*.
But I beg you, beware one man:
it's said he roams the Gallic land
where leggy ladies dance can-cans,
half Depardieu, half Jackie Chan...

At roadside *aires* outside Dieppe
he waits to give the tourists gip
with soggy roll-up on his lip —
and a firm grip:
it's Jean-Claude Gendarme.

You'd better come a-bearing cash
or he might kick your *rosbif* ass.
His temper even dwarfs his 'tache
(and it's a massive 'tache):
Jean-Claude Gendarme.

His *va va vroom* is overplayed,
he makes Le Pen look rather staid,
on human rights he's slightly vague:
call the Hague!
on Jean-Claude Gendarme.

It's *au revoir* when his car hones in,
poxy Peugeot siren droning.
Your Louvre trip will need postponing.
Gid moaning!
Jean-Claude Gendarme.

'Cause you forgot your hi vis jacket
this journey's costing you a packet.
You wish you'd braved the Cornish traffic
and home spun fascists,
not Jean-Claude Gendarme.

Jean-Claude Gendarme, the garlic Dalek:
he'll spoil your trip away.
Your mother tongue? Jean-Claude don't *parle* it,
so bring your best Franglais!

All nonchalant at your car door,
he spits and quips *Mais non Monsieur.*
Jean-Claude you lost me at *Bonjour*!
Ne pas encore!
Up yours Delores!
Jean-Claude Gendarme.

They don't dole out the karma free
at tourist town *gendarmeries*.
His sense of humour's *très petit*.
Mais oui!
Jean-Claude Gendarme.

From twelve to four he takes his luncheon
but otherwise the law's his function.
Are you pleased to see me or is that a truncheon?
It was a truncheon.
Jean-Claude Gendarme.

All five foot three with horn-rimmed specs,
I doubt he gets *beaucoup de* sex.
Napoleon weren't that complex.
Les filles reject
Jean-Claude Gendarme.

But one's compelled to acquiesce
when Jean dons gloves and says undress.
Next year I'm going to Skegness.
Mais Yes!
Jean-Claude Gendarme.

The Ballad of Mr & Mrs P. Cartwright

Well, hello there, what have we here?
A ballad, my what fun!
I like the way they tend to go:
di-dum, di-dum, di-dum.
They're solid and predictable
like Little Harpingon.

And Little Harpingon is where
this ghastly tale unfolds.
You know the sort of place I mean.
It's got a church, it's old;
where Barbour, Agas, Trollope sagas
and Tiptree Jams are sold.

The sort of little country town
that London folk find pretty,
so Kirsty helps them find a house
at prices that are silly,
while Phil sets out to rustle-up
a crash-pad in the city.

It's here in Little Harpingon
the Cartwright's got all homey —
their third car was a Land Rover
to tow their daughter's pony.
They used to vote Conservative
but then they switched to Tony

and blow me, don't the years fly by,
the kids soon flew the nest.
The Cartwrights watched them graduate
dressed in their Sunday best:
Jemima's having babies now
and Ru's at RBS.

Predictably retirement came;
the firm threw Pete a do.
The chairman made a lovely speech
which touched him through and through.
Then he and Mrs Cartwright left
to try new avenues.

Their life became as golden as
a Richard Curtis rom-com.
She'd potter in the garden while
he'd test drive with his Tom Tom
and say to neighbours as he passed:
Great bit of kit this – got one?

Mere weeks into their reverie
Jemima came to call:
Enjoy your golden handshake Dad,
but just don't spend it all.
D'you know, when this place is mine
I might take down that wall

and get a windmill in the garden,

take the place off-grid.
Huh? Sorry mum, what's that? The china?
Think we'll just get rid.
Oh shit, I'm late for pilates,
you'll have to mind the kids!

With that the yummy mummy went
and left her parents reeling.
Then seconds later Rupert entered,
jabbing at the ceiling:
You want to keep an eye on this.
I've got a nasty feeling

there might be structural damage here
and I won't foot the bill.
It's bloody tough at RBS:
I only got a mill.
Oh yes, and by the way old boy
I need to see the will.

I might need some of my bit now.
Could we work some trick?
I've got some poor bitch up the spuff
and need to get her fixed.
But not right now — got to dash —
so maybe fax me it?

And here's the leaflet for that home.
He gave his dad a poke:

Your heart could pack up any day
and she's prime for a stroke.
Just promise you'll consider it.
Then Rupert left his folks.

Well, Peter Cartwright sighed and said:
We knew this day would come.
I think they call it karma
after what we did to Mum.
Camilla, pudding, please don't whimper:
trust me, they'll get none.

Behind his specs his cruel eyes slimmed,
he thumped his palsied fist.
Yes, darling, fetch the Bollinger
let's both get really pissed.
And grab that pad of Basildon Bond,
we'll make a shopping list:

a massage table, training bikes,
some botox for our faces,
a suit for me, a hat for you,
a weekend at the races.
Golly, this Bolly folly's jolly —
let's buy a few more cases.

A cottage in the Hebrides,
perhaps a country pub;
let's hire an alcoholic chef

to make the standard grub
and slowly drink our profits till
the place is boarded up.

Yes! Let's go trekking in the Andes!
Shall we get a boat?
I could run for parliament.
I doubt I'll get the votes
but I hear the PR's very dear —
so let's least get a quote?

So Mr and Mrs P Cartwright
flashed their reckless streak
and branded Luton vans arrived
with gadgets and antiques.
Expensive hobbies were begun
then dumped within a week.

The children's former bedrooms
housed the flutes they never played,
plus dusty golf clubs, racing bikes
and dinner sets and lathes.
You've heard of "affluenza," right?
Well, this was "afflu-AIDS."

But though they tried their very best
their credit wouldn't taper.
The Cartwrights were quite comfortable
a year into their caper

until one morning Pete let out
a shriek over his paper:

Camilla, look, it says right here
Ru's bank is at the limit —
it says it's staffed by nincompoops
whose policies are gimmicks.
It's going under any day —
let's throw our money in it.

An anxious thirty minutes passed
and Pete put down the phone:
the broker needed talking round,
I didn't like his tone.
Eventually though he saw sense —
our legacy is blown.

By dinner time, the bank was down;
reporters made a fuss
by interviewing blokes like Ru
who just said: *Don't blame us!*
The treasury should bail us out,
it's damned ridiculous!

As repo men in cheap grey suits
made lists from floor to floor,
the Cartwrights clinked their champagne flutes
and let off loud guffaws
and when the place was emptied out

they closed their kitchen door

and walked through Little Harpingon
for several voiceless hours,
stopping every now and then
to pick each other flowers.
Then when the sunset fell on them
they climbed the church's tower.

And shoeless on the battlements,
half-lit by orange light,
Peter and Camilla Cartwright
stood as man and wife —
till after many minutes there
they stepped into the night.

But hold it folks, don't shed your tears,
this wasn't suicide:
the church's tower in Harpingon
is thirty-four foot high.
Those cunning, spendthrift baby-boomers
were only paralyzed.

In hospital for decades more
the Cartwrights lay quite still
so no-one ever knew if they'd
intended to be killed —
though Rupert swore they winked at him
when he came to pay their bill.

The Billionaire Princess

Her mother made her wear a rod of steel
along her spine, like one of Daddy's rails.
A single track, an extra in a deal
in which an ancient magic was for sale.
A straight-up swap in which each father won —
the Yankies got to join the sacred club,
the English got their fortunes back, a son
if they were lucky. No-one spoke of love.
So, still a teen, she married for a title;
she bore the duke an heir and gazed at ponds,
each stifled day a series of recitals
of age-old protocol and gilded bonds.
A perfect portrait model, rigid, still;
a flower drying on a window sill.

The Royal Wedding, 1947

They say she had to save up all her rations,
for fabric like much else had gotten dearer;
but average clothing coupons couldn't fashion
a gown like Botticelli's *Primavera*

or trade for twenty thousand US pearls,
buy Winterthur silk or a myrtle sprig.
Still, princesses are not like other girls
and this was not an ordinary gig.

A cold November's day, just clear of war,
the country missing one from every dozen;
at last a thing to do your make-up for:
Elizabeth was married to her cousin.

And proud among the jasmine and the pheasants,
the Russian fringe tiara from Queen Mary,
the gross of gloves and countless silver presents,
there stood a three-tier cake from Castle Cary

that half the town had rubber-necked to see.
They stirred the mix and gossiped of the gold,
then later, tuned into the BBC
to hear a real-life fairy tale unfold.

And still the baker's daughter tells the tale;

she doesn't care that some might find it tragic —
a commoner indulging in her pale,
warm thoughts of being touched by Royal magic.

And often I'm the one to rail and slur:
equality's the thing, not Kings and Queens!
But when I see how much this meant to her
it makes me hush my talk of guillotines.

For Radio

I think of you as telly's older sister —
the old maid of the airwaves, staunch and true.
Your stroppy sibling takes a better picture
but thinking men would rather drink with you.
They say you help them drown their midnight sorrow
with arguments or strange progressive noise
and don't think any less of them tomorrow
when switching to your sober, breezy voice.
They love your thousand-strong impersonations
and how you know the answer to most things,
your whispered prayers in corners of the nation
and how you raise their spirits when you sing.
They hear themselves in you, in cars, at home.
You seem to say: *we're none of us alone.*

Jeremy, Who Drew Penises on Everything

Meet Jeremy, a sporty youth,
whose pressing need to leave some proof
of his existence on this earth
would cause his friends much glee and mirth.
They'd shake and howl at Jez's feats
and claim his presence quite a treat —
as sure as Welshmen like to sing,
young Jez drew cocks on everything.

On books, on blackboards, desks and chairs,
he carved them into Camembert,
he scribbled them on toilet doors,
left penile prints in chests of drawers;
he crayoned dongs on Bibles and
drew tiny ones upon his hand
until no stretch of schoolyard wall
was free from Jez's cartoon balls.

All day he sketched crude diagrams,
drew shlongs upon his toast with jam,
arranged his sausage with his eggs
to emulate between the legs.
While later in some muggy class
he'd pounce upon the steamed-up glass
and then to whoops from all his mates
he'd make his work ejaculate.

Yes, all the boys were straight-up fans
of Jeremy's artistic hand
and masters, far from scolding him,
would praise the young lad for his vim
and feisty creativity
(not one suggested therapy).
The teachers saw no real malice
in Jezzer when he sketched a phallus.

At home his parents did the same,
refused to dole out any blame,
although their walls were covered in
a thousand sketchy ding-a-lings
and Jez had scared off friends and lodgers
with likenesses of spurting todgers.
No, mum & dad just praised the boy
for drawing willies on his toys.

And Jezzer with the naughty pen
grew up and then became PM!
And now that boy who liked to draw
has led us into countless wars.
The moral of this ghastly tale:
beware of cocksure, thrusting males.
For blokes like Jez, if free and able,
will always put their dicks on tables.

SCANDAL!

Consider this — the grainy long lens snap,
the shocked CAPS LOCK, the exclamation mark,
the leading light of tinsel town who's papped
walking his dog at midnight in the park,
the naughty businessman who likes more slap
than tickle and the brandy-loosened nark.
Yes, SCANDAL's what I speak of and it's true:
we Brits, it seems, have little else to do

than coo and wince and bite our bottom lips
or tell a 5 Live phone-in: *It's disgraceful* —
bazookas fired yawning from our hips.
We lap it up and then say, *It's distasteful
the way the media pries and nigh-on rips
through people's lives, it's bordering on hateful.*
But you forget, you pillars with the hump,
the tale of Rupert and Minerva Crump.

Huh? Rupert and Minerva who? You say.
Well naturally I've changed their names of course,
one has to be so careful nowadays,
my poesy's far too sensitive for court.
And Steve, my publicist, is going grey;
injunctions on this verse won't help his cause.
But rest assured the contents of this story
are true, and it concerns a horrid Tory.

Oh, not more Tory bashing Luke, you cry!
Well, trust me folks, the Tories aren't my quarry;
it just so happened Rupert caught my eye.
The fact he's one of that lot shouldn't worry
you; my politics won't make me lie.
And should I bend the truth I shan't be sorry;
corruption swings from my satiric rope.
If you don't like it, read some Wendy Cope.

So, Rupert Crump — let's put him on your maps:
he claimed to be "just one of life's eccentrics";
a reedy, thin-lipped, gormless sort of chap.
At Cambridge while his peers got stoned to Hendrix
he trod the boards and doffed his velvet cap
to right-wing ideology, a blend which
would serve him well. Tebbit with added fizz,
the Mike Yarwood of Young Conservatives.

The rest at best is clichéd so we'll race:
the Bar, of course, then greasing-up the right
gnarled dinosaur at Smith's Square, then a brace
of failed elections, till one muggy night
he finally experienced the taste
of power he so longed for when a might
of haughty housewives pleased with life in Cheshire
sent Rupert off to Westminster, with pleasure.

And with him went his bride of not a week:
Minerva — curvy, bossy, doctor's daughter.

More jolly hockey-sticks than London chic,
a good home-counties catch and Rupert caught her.
A pre-existing member of the clique,
an MP's secretary, which had taught her
how to be the perfect Tory wife,
and *that*, she thought, would always be her life.

For this was '83 and Thatcher's reign
looked stiffer than a swift kick in the balls;
the well-worn line of *Necessary pain*
was bellowed from the dispatch box with gall.
The northern towns were bled, the state was drained,
the chances of a Kinnock charge were small.
And in this brave new pinstripe-plated world
the champers flowed for Rupert and his girl.

He made his Commons mark with plucky speeches,
all anti child-support and immigration.
The poor, he claimed, were lazy, luckless leeches,
and cuts would cure the market's constipation.
His ideology made Friedrich Nietzsche's
look more like Desmond Tutu's Rainbow Nation.
And while the country cowered from this hate,
hors d'oeuvres were served Chez Crump to Britain's great.

On TV screens all gawdy hue and square
they dined away a decade in this manner.
From Kelvin's POOFS OF POP to SUN BACKS BLAIR
an endless, listless dance under the banner

of nasty-party-rich-with-none-to-spare:
exterminate the state and *Sing Hosanna*.
I know, I know, I know I'm getting partial,
but trust me please, this fellow was an arsehole.

They made him Minister — of course they did —
there's nothing like an arsehole for that job
but Rupert found it hard to keep a lid
on all the rubbish spewing from his gob.
He'd rather just play parliamentary wit
and seek another way to earn a bob.
Another way to keep life smelling sweet —
so Rupert traded on his Commons seat.

Now, friends, before you judge, consider this.
Poor Crump was up to nothing very new:
Lloyd George and Churchill stuffed their pudgy fists!
You don't believe me? Look it up, it's true!
Still, stuff like that propels a journo's wrist
and soon enough some Bolshy lefties knew.
They splashed it all across *The Grauniad*
and CASH FOR QUESTIONS? — well, it just looks bad.

His financier was Tariq Al Atrash,
the owner of a famous British shop;
as deals go, the move was somewhat rash,
for Al Atrash's cake hole rarely stopped.
Inevitable he'd blab about the cash —
and so he did, whoops missus, call the cops!

And so began the cries of *Vicious Libel!*
I'll swear on it! Good sir, pass me that Bible!

But Crump, ex-prancing actor, knew his Wilde —
when libel cases fail, your problems start.
A Westminster committee's much more mild,
duplicitous and well-skilled in the art
of pardoning its own. But don't be riled
what happened next will truly warm the heart —
before MPs could do their limp inspection
Crump had to fight a general election.

Democracy, that boobie, has her days
and this was surely up there with the best!
A TV newsman, name of Peter Bray,
self-righteous to the last and smugly dressed
from head to toe in white, strode into the fray
and promptly took the seat for Cheshire West.
A kind of shorthand for the Tory's slump;
the lefties crowed: *Oh, were you up for Crump.*

But one good thing to come from all the pain:
Minerva's fifteen minutes in the lights.
Her snipes at Bray had spiced-up Crump's campaign
and got her on the goggle-box most nights.
She'd earned herself a hackneyed sort of fame:
the battleaxe who's spoiling for a fight.
You can't accuse the press of being varied:
women — they're either sexy or they're scary.

So, as the century which gave us Einstein,
computers and The Beatles sucked its last,
the scandal-sullied Crumps were out of fine wines
and using up their old friends' grace quite fast.
In lieu of politics they went for primetime;
it left the stiffs of Westminster aghast.
This former Tory MP and his wife
living the glamour model's sort of life.

They went on TV quizzes and they laughed
about the charges levelled at their door.
Did Panto in the Midlands where they arsed
about on stage like bouncy Labradors.
They poured their hearts whenever they were asked,
in ways the good and proper would deplore!
They took the scandal clinging to their name
and spun it into cash and easy fame.

And true to form, we Brits were glued to them.
We tutted, sure, but still we slowed and gawped.
They sold out at the Fringe and yearly penned
a slew of articles the tabloids bought.
For while we hate a liar, in the end
it's well trumped by our love of a good sport.
Embracing what is trying to devour you
can often mean that thing just re-empowers you.

And thus the meeja did for Ru and Min.
In interviews they never moaned or whined,

just trotted out this bouncy bit of spin:
We've left the sham of politics behind
for the real world of show business. Cue grin.
And that of course will always be the line
it has to be, but what I want to know
is how they function when the film crews go?

On dark nights of the soul are thighs still slapped?
Is singing for your supper still so gay?
And were they really pleased their phones weren't hacked
'cause no-one thinks them grand enough these days?
Or do they gaze at photos feeling trapped
like phantoms; do they beg and cry and pray
and wake in cold sweats wishing it untrue?
Oh Rupert love, oh love what did you do!?

And if they do, is that what they deserve?
Is SCANDAL democratic punishment?
A dish of last resorts the public serves
when law is limp or slack and judges bent?
Or is it tyranny with added verve,
a modern noose to ease our discontent?
Well, I don't know, perhaps it's just the drool
Narcissus spills while staring at the pool?

Bloody Hell, It's Barbara!

The tits that crashed a thousand cars,
a hot knife through the city's bars,
full complement of facial scars —
Bloody Hell, it's Barbara!

All thunder thighs and lightning hair,
resplendent in her underwear,
I want that one, it isn't fair!
Bloody Hell, it's Barbara!

Well versed in dark romantic arts,
she feeds each night on fledgling hearts,
indeed on any private parts —
Bloody Hell, it's Barbara!

Bloody Hell! OMG! *Sacre Bleu!* It's Barbara!
As sumptuous and stylish as a Gothic candelabra.
I want to dock my dinghy in the safety of your harbour.
A bidet full of ice would not begin to cool my ardour.

The kind of broad that gangsters rate,
the type to make kings abdicate,
enough to turn the Navy straight —
Bloody Hell, it's Barbara!

Boudicca but soaked in liquor,
tactless as a bumper sticker,
Oh la la, my dicky ticker!
Bloody Hell, it's Barbara!

Think boozy busty nightclub rep
meets Super Nanny all windswept,
I think I need the naughty step —
Bloody hell, it's Barbara!

Bloody Hell! What's all this? Free Tibet! It's Barbara.
Imagine Mrs Robinson, if she had come from Scarborough.
She twists herself around you like clematis on an arbour.
In every English town a fella's weeping to his barber.
Bloody hell, it's Barbara!
Bloody hell, it's Barbara!

Her love is aching arteries,
her night caps nips of anti-freeze,
my sonnets bawdy journalese,
as sure as pepper makes you sneeze
and Russians come from overseas,
I want you Barbara, can I please,
I need to hear you pant and wheeze,
I'm begging you, I'm on my knees,
just give me all your STDs —
Bloody hell, it's Barbara

Bloody hell! Stop the clocks! Bring out your dead! It's Barbara.
I want to take a tit-bit from your cool and gloomy larder.
I think I'm at the end now 'cause the rhymes are getting harder,
so here it is, the chorus line
just shout it out one final time —
Bloody hell, it's Barbara!

The Rise and Fall of Dudley Livingstone

Meet dear old Dudley Livingstone, respectable and hoary,
a little bit of Jack the Lad, a pinch of Jackanory.
A lineage of hunts and shoots, a manor with a maze,
though savvy Dudley kept hush-hush his yomping Eton days

and kept to shooting off his pen in periodicals,
where jingoistic bingo cards in plummy doggerel
were mixed with pleas to save the arts and calls for going green
which meant when he said, *Send 'em back*, it sounded less extreme.

Oh blessed is the cyclist — he shall inherit Kent.
A poetry recital is the public pound well spent.
A thought occurred to me last night, why don't we castrate yobs?
An awful lot of Poles about, I hear they want your jobs.

His crumbly vocal chords were often on the BBC;
his jokes on *Woman's Hour* made Jenni Murray snort her tea.
And chaps like that are wasted in the private sector tent,
so Dudley got the call one day: *Prepare for Parliament.*

And soon a by-election seat in safest Tory Surrey,
where multiculturalism is *going for a curry*.
The kind of place *The Mail* thrives in all its gruesome shrillness:
Oh goodness, we're not bigots, but being gay's an illness.

The type who cheer for wickets in the dappled English sun

thought Dudley just the ticket so they ticked the box marked CON.

He made his mark in Parliament a firmly anti stance,
reactionary but edgy and familiar at a glance:

Dear Dudley was the member who would call for anti-sleaze.
Dear Dudley was the member who would shout *Let's save the trees!*
Dear Dudley called for closing mosques: *And why not burn them too!*
but always made us giggle on *Have I Got News For You.*

So people didn't mind about the racial insurrections
because he stumbled on his words and had contrived inflections.
His hair was always messy and he'd never zip his flies.
Why, he was posh and silly, quite incapable of lies.

Dear Dud had mastered anti-spin: the more he looked confused,
the more he could be prejudiced and always be excused.
So when the summer rolled around the party gave permission
and Dudley found himself as Leader of the Opposition.

From there to Number Ten, where Dudley made himself at home;
he annexed parts of Brighton, locked transsexuals in the Dome,
put armed police in precincts where the working classes shopped,
imposed custodial sentences on youths that glottal-stopped.

And always had an answer that sat well with Middle Britain.
He joked around with Clarkson, keeping Fifty Quid Man smitten.
He hired a murky Murdoch stooge to clean up any mess
and hid behind cheap references when dealing with the press:

— Prime Minister, will you explain the atom bomb on Gaza?
— Oh bloody hell, not that again, here's me with Lady Gaga.

With blokey jokes and lifestyle spreads he had our admiration;
good natured gaffes in chat show chats mask darker implications.

But then one foggy London morn his world came crashing down:
the kissed and blabbered nights of vice with Arabella Brown.
His thick-thighed dominatrix sold her story to the press,
her fifty shades of sleaze filled every page of *The Express*:

Oh Dudley's such an animal, he's naughty, he's a giggle.
He likes a golden shower when he's dressed as Iggle Piggle!

For Dudley, as a married man, this was a moral blight.
The Mail can take a holocaust but *Cheating just ain't right.*
And now the spell had been undone, the papers got officious;
the horrid things that Dud had done seem all the more suspicious.

They hounded him from Downing Street without a second look.
They cursed him for a year or two but then they bought his book
and with a dewy eye recalled his gift to play the fool.
Oh what a pity, they remarked, *he had to break the rules.*

Luke's Got a Joke

Imagine a pub on a bright afternoon
as warm autumn sunlight is cast through the room —
a second pint started, the discourse fermented,
a large group of friends feeling vaguely contented.

But damn all this chit-chat, for Luke is not in it!
He's had no attention for nearly a minute!
His lips start to quiver, his head starts to dip,
he topples his pint as he stands and lets rip:

Luke's got a joke!
Luke's got a story!
Look out for his humorous lines about Tories!
Luke's got a viewpoint, so perk up your ears.
He's really quite droll when he's had a few beers.

Let's cut to a wake and some folksy guitar,
the subject of death trumping Luke's repertoire,
which simply won't do — so he bellows the question:
Who here likes a good Austin Powers impression?

Before they can stop him he's poofed up his hair,
he's stuck out his teeth and said *Yeah, baby, yeah*
till everyone's squirming and forcing a smile,
wishing someone had breastfed Luke as a child.

Luke's got a joke!
Luke's got a punchline!
All of it fresh from the literary frontline.
Luke's got opinions — from headlines to sport.
He's not listening to you, he's just planning retorts.

Let's visit Chez Luke where ol' Luke and his missus
are plying their guests with some coffee and biscuits.
Here's Luke holding court like some self-obsessed teen;
he collects his applause and then exits the scene.

A friend takes the chance to recount her weekend, though
as her witty yarn starts to reach its crescendo
a noise from the doorway and all turn to see
young Luke crying: *I done asparagus wee!*

Luke's got a joke!
Luke's got a gift
for writing himself into those urban myths.
Remember that weird thing, that one off, that fluke?
Believe it or not, that all happened to Luke.

He's great at the voices, sit back, watch him act —
it's like Eddie Izzard is here in the flat!
Oh no Luke, you don't come across as a twat.
Do your Mrs Doyle. That's brilliant, that.

No Luke, don't stop Luke, we're keen to hear more;
it's better when you say "Don't mention the war!"

Forget that night out at the Comedy Store;
we'd rather hear Luke do some Blackadder 4.

Luke's got a joke!
Luke's got a gag
repeated verbatim from bad fashion mags!
Luke's got a verdict — shut up, let him rave —
and then when he's finished, give him what he craves.

If you see some students enthralled in their lesson,
a couple of lovers just stealing a second,
a group of beer buddies just chewing the fat,
a brace of old dears going yakkety-yak,

be sure Luke's approaching these charming vignettes,
preparing to act out the 'Dead Parrot Sketch'
or offer some line from the cavernous jaws
of a life that's just echo and hollow applause.

At 4.48am Sentinel_poet wrote:

I type in fevered silence in the night,
defending fragile poesy from this blight
of ballad rap and mawkish sentiment,
the brackish sludge, the reeking sediment
of media-friendly, level-entry dross,
stercoral whimsy, gauchely caked in gloss,
accessible and clumsy rhyming faeces:
at this I aim my pixelated theses.
Beware, blithe poetasters, for I slog
each night to slay your curdled claptrap on my blog.

Indeed on any page where doggerel lingers
no CAPTCHA code's too nimble for my fingers.
These noble pinkies wield enormous power:
look on them, bunkum bards, and duly cower.
They'll dole you out a witty rubbishing:
Get back where you belong — *self-publishing!*
I right the wrongs of writing gone arthritic
by those who seem to lack an inner critic,
but always save the tersest of my scorn
for harlequins who stand up in pubs and perform!

Those egotists! I tell my Twitterati;
Who said these half-wit boobies could be arty?
You have to go on courses, pay your dues!
You have to polish Sean O'Brien's shoes!

Just like I did. You have to play the game
before the great and good will learn your name
and if they never do — well, that's just tough.
It took those cliquey snobs quite long enough
to notice me, I'm still not in their club.
Each year a list is published *and* each year a snub!

Can no-one see the subtle Esperanto
contained within the twenty-thousand cantos
I've published (free of charge!) upon my blog?
Our noble art is headed for the dogs!
A duel attack: by rhyming stand-up comics
who wouldn't know a haiku from a sonnet,
and tasteless masons backed by fawning hoards
who cook the books and fix all the awards.
While I, bereft of laughter and of prizes,
must fight them all each night, until the sun rises.

Mondeo Man

Last week I walked through Maidenhead suburbs.
Good old boys stooping to check their tyre pressures,
mums hauling kids in car seats like they're shopping,
bins standing to attention by well-kept lawns

neat as parade grounds, a Valium hush
and a blue door that made me think of a lido
I visited before we were together,
before the life we made swelled in your belly.

I walked there every evening for a week
and watched the lido, jutting out to sea;
I ate my chips and imagined it crammed
full of tan-lined, knobbly British bodies

and wondered why my new romantic life
at mic stands felt perpetually out of season.
Yet last week in Maidenhead (of all places)
I felt strangely at ease with normality.

There was a time I'd walk through here scolding,
tutting, talking in quotes and references;
too clever for nice weather and caravans;
too clever, too smart to be taken in.

Who'd want 2.4 children? I'd say,
in visor and asymmetrical fringe.
Or, *What dickhead works nine to five?*
slurping spaghetti hoops straight from the tin.

Disgusted at people who had settled,
shaking my dust till my fingers bleed,
shaking my dust till it got up my nose
and I'd cough and sneeze for weeks on end.

Maybe it's because I drive a Mondeo
and have started wearing trousers that fit
that I've realised that we do not die
with our affectations; if anything we live.

You can't just be what other people aren't.
You can't plot your life like a misery memoir
or wait to hang smiles on the whims of strangers
or put out to tender your dictionary entry.

Ambition used to hunt me like a zombie
till I'd throw it bits of my poems like flesh;
I'd stare at my inbox hitting refresh;
I'd get places early just to catch my breath.

But now, I think of those ruddy-cheeked weavers
in lopsided seventeenth century towns
who when they'd earned enough money that week
declared a Saint's Day and went down the pub.

Centuries from the boy on his Blackberry
at Broadcasting House writing poems to go,
crying and wanking on fringe theatre stages,
twanging his id like a diddely-bo.

Motorways from a boy in a visor
trying to make it all mean something more,
wistfully staring at a swimming pool:
the lido is a metaphor for... for... for...

Last week I walked through Maidenhead suburbs
and though I knew I wouldn't find an ending,
I realised that I've learnt something new:
that sometimes it's ok just to blend in.

Another Grotty Holiday

When I tell folk I'm off on tour
it tends to prompt respectful awe.
I know they're thinking Spinal Tap
and snorting gak from ladies' laps,
or least some City Lights-type scene,
when really I'm in Milton Keynes
or standing in a men's latrine
whilst halfway up the A15
as lorries duel on carriageways —
Another Grotty Holiday.

No M&Ms in brandy glasses,
bohemians with backstage passes;
no fluffy towels or high-class hookers,
just very worried theatre bookers
who've all turned prematurely grey,
who look upset and turn away
when I ask what I've sold that day,
who wring their hands and shyly say:
There's ten out there, and seven paid —
Another Grotty Holiday.

Spend nasty polystyrene lunchtimes
in cities you once used as punchlines:
Come to Preston! Visit Croydon!
See those rough men? Best avoid them.

Why play Rome, when you've got Leeds,
a dressing room where roaches breed,
a fee that's less than you'd agreed
and half the crowd are blokes in tweed?
When friendly bombs have gone astray —
Another Grotty Holiday.

The slip-road waits at Dartford's toll
are making in-roads to your soul.
Suicide windows, mocking moon.
The salesman died, you got his room.
To be is not to B&B
(especially when it smells of wee);
to spend your nights with Pay TV
to wake up every day and see
your tea things on a plastic tray,
you overlook the motorway.
So here's your key, enjoy your stay —
Another Grotty Holiday.

Clean Slate

You cheated on your girlfriend
so now she's at my place bitching with my wife
while I carry your life
down staircases in torn plastic bags.

We load my car with lever arch files
in boxes meant for oranges.
It's shabby. These things are not you:
the pink plastic backpack, the forgotten fleece,
The Tesseract by Alex Garland.
We shift unloved items
through the still night.

You show me your new house,
its Bond villain windows
and too many chairs.
You tell me about your new girlfriend.
She's American. Maybe you'll go and live there.

I get it.
The attraction of starting again.
I talk up a clean slate as we lug boxes
and reassemble shelves. You toast cut ties.
Until the sweat starts to dry,
until it's time for me to skulk back to my still life
and leave you hanging curtains.

Weekday Dad

Like most of my left-leaning, liberal colleagues,
I'm proud when announcing my feminist bent;
the well-rehearsed speeches I honed while at college
have got me in knickers from Kendal to Kent.

Oh wow, that's so true, yeah, I'm such a supporter
of feminist causes... Simone de Beauvoir?
My god, that's uncanny, she's my favourite author!
Do you need assistance with burning your bra?

And don't think me sexist, I just had the horn.
I loathed all that lad-maggish crass repartee
but issues like these cut much deeper than porn.
You see, life, it turns out, was much simpler for me
than for girls who were faced with the Catch 22
of slut-walks and burkas and glass-ceiling-ed jobs,
linguistic subservience, *Maxim* and *Zoo*
and all of that bottled-up envy of nobs. (Joke!)

At sixteen I just didn't get Women's Lib;
the feminist texts were a means to an end.
I tried but was clueless and likely to rib:
I'm not sexist, some of my best women are friends.

But slowly it dawned that away from the clamour,
the boobs and the marches, the glitz and the bars,

equality battles are fought without glamour
in kitchens and bedrooms, in classrooms and cars.

Now older, with no need for bogus ID,
a father, no less, to a two year-old lad,
I'm putting my time where my mouth used to be:
they know me in this town as...

Weekday Dad.
With my sidekick — Dribble Boy.

The day starts at half five with Dribble Boy's yelping
(his cranium wedged through the bars of his cot)
and ends with that petulant toddler pelting
poor me with his tea while I line up the shots.

It turns out that being a dab hand at poesy
will scarcely equip you to wipe a child's bum.
Being able to critique *A Ring-Ring-A-Rosy*
will not mean he doesn't just scream for his mum.

Yes, stand back, don't panic, it's dad to the rescue!
He's always so eager to clean you and dress you!
You've drawn on the wall? Oh how charming, oh bless you!
A glint in your eye that reminds of Ceauşescu.

By half eight I'm locked in a battle of wills
with someone who isn't yet able to speak;
no wonder these housewives are all on the pills

surrounded by psychos with cute, chubby cheeks.

No sweetie, not that please, it's Daddy's degree!
No, not in the potty dear, that's where you wee!
It's not that I need it, it's just that I, gee,
that's pretty symbolic — you've satirised me.

We're mobile by nine and I'm bent like a hag
ineptly maneuvering baby and pram,
and time throws a tantrum, insisting it lags
as I trudge round in circles like one of the damned.

Then just when I'm thinking it can't get much worse,
just when I'm ready to call for my nurse,
just when I'm starting to dream of the hearse,
I see them approach, but they've seen me first:

Competitive middle-class mummies from hell,
all former high flyers and boy can't you tell,
their days colour-coded and run from Excel,
their offspring are spotless and ready to spell:

Xavier's reading at age seven level;
he's only just three, yet so smart when he talks.
But enough about my lot, who's this little devil?
I love his weird eye, and his odd limpy walk.
Oh bless him, oh love him, he's so sort of... feral.
Just look at the cute way he's eating that chalk.

And you, she says, turning her neat eyes on me,
so good of you, giving your partner a rest!
Your Daddy's so brave, oh it's so good to see!
My husband can't even get our children dressed!

And sure there's a part of me far from immune
from massively trading off staying at home.
I'm such a new man — cue drink soiree swoons —
Yes, here's me and him, I say swiping my phone.

But that there's the thing at the heart of the issue:
all parenting's tough whether female or male.
We've all left the house without nappies or tissues,
we've all gone to bed with that feeling we've failed.

But women can't show off or boast they selected
raising their kids over getting ahead;
despite all the hot air, it's still just expected,
like changing your second name after you've wed.

I want to explain that I'm not seeking praise
or, failing that, just do a bunk down the road.
I'm quietly steaming, still locked in her gaze,
but Dribble Boy stops me before I explode.

He chooses this moment to headbutt a wall
and I know he's upset but the look of surprise
is priceless and perfect as he starts to bawl.
He reaches for me with his mum in his eyes.

And these moments stay with us, wallpaper the brain;
quotidian splendor that spreads as it splinters;
a near perfect rainbow one spots from a train;
the pink of the crab apple after the winter.

They fortify me against 6am starts,
the lack of applauding (despite all my brilliance);
they give me a peace I've not known in my heart
for such a long time and though only a billionth
of all of the tears and the ear-bursting screams,
they help tip the scales to somewhere near equal,
countering tantrums and stand-offs and scenes —
they've even compelled us to work on a sequel.

And I know these moments aren't just for prime carers
and working dads catch them on snatched Saturdays
but those seem more polished and certainly rarer.
I guess I'm just saying I prefer it this way.

A143

The Waveney has burst its banks again.
The Earsham water meadows: tiny seas
protesting at their walls. I put the peddle
to the floor. The Transit coughs its lungs
then eats the Harleston bypass like it's dirt.

Today's a day for dumping and collecting,
for flinging black bin liners into skips
and loading up the van with eBay finds;
our snapped and tatty plastic junk replaced
with solid wardrobe oak and yawning chests.

I clock two hundred blissful miles like this,
tracing time along North Suffolk's spine
past mounds of frozen beets and real ale pubs,
past Redenhall's resplendent hilltop church,
near holy in the January sun.

The Ballad of Raoul Moat

All my life I wanted death,
hence the reason I took risks;
made the worst of enemies,
did the things I did.

And so to June in twenty ten,
well-baked and stinking hot,
an oil slick spreading up the Gulf
and Britain newly shot

of Darling, Brown and Mandelson;
let's go to Durham Jail,
where lads from Tyne and Wearside
who have ventured off the rails

are sent, where Ronnie Kray did bird,
where Ian Brady's boasts
would echo round Victorian walls,
where Myra Hindley's ghost

is said to haunt the F Wing lags,
where time's a two tonne weight,
where Private Brian Chandler
was hung in fifty-eight.

And there in bastard, sticky June,
all hunched up in the haze,
a prisoner called Raoul Moat
is counting down the days.

A beefed-up panel-beater, sometime
bouncer, arborist,
his poxy past pock-marked with crimes,
a life of tears and fists.

Banged-up for eighteen measly weeks
for clobbering a child,
he hugs his knees, his forehead drips,
his thoughts are black, rank, wild

and treacle-thick, half drenched in 'roids.
His cranium's well crammed
imagining that filthy pig,
that copper with his Sam.

For she's a bitch, a slag, a cunt.
For she is filth and sin.
And when Raoul Moat walks free from here
he's going to do her in.

> *All my life I wanted death,*
> *hence the reason I took risks;*
> *made the worst of enemies,*
> *did the things I did.*

For six years Sam had felt his hand
since she was just sixteen.
She'd had his kid so she was his
but then law intervened

and set her free, she ended it
but knew he'd try to stop her;
so terrified she told a lie,
said she was with a copper.

And by the time that Moat was out,
the lie had slicked in him;
a black and oily hatred
weighing heavy in his limbs.

This cruel injustice fitted him.
Raoul Moat was used to it.
The mirror showed a victim
they kept face down in the shit.

The burly British underdog,
the disenfranchised thug;
Blitzkrieged with stuff he couldn't have
and wrecked on muscle drugs.

Raoul Moat romanticised himself.
It wasn't very hard.
The noble savage cuckolded,
the stuff of ballad bards.

Convinced himself he had no choice:
a gruesome trick or treat.
He took his sawn-off shotgun
to a sleepy Gateshead street

at 3am, when madness prowls
and stalks around your head.
He killed the man he thought a cop;
he left his girl for dead,

her liver ruptured, stomach burst —
what could he do but run?
But very soon the word was out
and then the hunt was on.

All my life I wanted death,
hence the reason I took risks;
made the worst of enemies,
did the things I did.

And Fleet Street, with its penchant
for a manhunt and a murder,
made Raoul Moat a frontpage splash
from *Mirror* to *Observer*.

The bleached-out passport photo
with the psycho, steroid stare;
the breathy editorials
that warned good folk, beware —

Raoul Moat was tabloid dynamite;
the papers drooled for more —
a shot of Tarantino
with a can of Geordie Shore.

And Moaty duly gave them what
they'd all been waiting for.
He seized upon a squad car
and he walked up to the door,

shot PC Rathband in the eye
to further square his score.
Oh how the wire buzzed that day;
oh how the newsrooms roared.

'Cause here we had a hunt-a-thon,
a real time movie reeling:
Another take please, Mr Moat,
and this time, Raoul, with feeling.

And Moaty gave the goods again —
a fifty-six page letter:
his victim spiel, his love for Sam
and why he had to get her.

Confessional and laced with fear,
from Desperation Row,
as mawkish as the sobbing kids
from TV talent shows.

His vanity and loneliness,
his sorrow, dark and grim;
it struck a chord with thousands
and they sympathised with him

All my life I wanted death,
hence the reason I took risks;
made the worst of enemies,
did the things I did.

And so, against a chorus
of a million op-ed sages,
a popcorn-toting public and
some *Go Raoul!* Facebook pages,

the cops stepped up their hunt across
the bitter and sparse hills,
pulled bobbies off their local beats,
and even hired Bear Grylls

to track Moat down to Rothbury
where once upon a time
they sung of blackleg mining men
who broke the picket line.

And here, word of a storm drain
on the outskirts of the town
soon brought the paparazzi and
the Sky News choppers down,

so everyone could tune in live
on tellies, tubes and feeds,
as armed police closed in around,
the man upon his knees,

his own gun pointed at his throat;
a desperate stalemate
as journos madly tapped their phones
and coppers offered bait.

His friends were fetched to talk him down
but still Moat held his ground;
when Gazza pitched up with some grub,
it ceased to be profound

and morphed into a pantomime —
surreal and almost funny.
The public got their spectacle.
The papers made more money.

But some, I fancy, felt for him,
this lonely, beaten figure,
his world in bits around him when
he finally pulled the trigger.

All my life I wanted death,
hence the reason I took risks;
made the worst of enemies,
did the things I did.

So breathe, the dreadful thing is done.
What tragedy! What pity!
The action men reporters went
a-tweeting to the city

and left the folk in Rothbury
with trampled lawns and greens,
who tidied up their town and left
some flowers at the scene.

Police began their paperwork,
enquiries commenced,
and even politicians
who are usually on the fence

got stuck in. David Cameron,
our newly-voted chief,
he stood up in the Commons
and although he kept it brief

condemned the folk who'd set up pages
rooting for Raoul Moat,
the sort of folk who hate the cops,
the sort who do not vote,

the people so devoid of heroes
killers fill that role,
a long, long way from London,
familiar with the dole.

They didn't even pause for breath
before they started hating
and wagging bony fingers
at the Raoul Moats in the making.

While blinded, PC David Rathband
pushed away his wife,
enclaved in sheer-black solitude,
he broke and took his life.

This ballad has no heroes,
its tune is not so hot;
the chances are it won't be heard
above the tabloid's shots:

the blunt, cathartic bullet storms
that state some folk are scum,
that certain things can only be
made better with a gun.

The Meek

Stepney, seven PM
pre-weekend beers,
extended sesh.
Meek Drew meets gentle Beth.
He resembles Dexter Fletcher.
Her eyes gelled green —
she's Renee Zellweger meets Betty Spencer,
svelte yet sexless.

Hey sweets, he creeps,
pets her tender flesh,
pecks her sherbet cheek —
she merely *tee-hee-hees*
then screeches *Feed me Drew*!

They enter The Ten Bells
(est. seventeen-seventy-three)
where he spends freely —
he gets beer,
she Red Cherry Reef (the effervescent refreshment).
They select entrées,
then the beef.

She tells Drew she seeks self-betterment.
She's well Zen.
Every week she stretches, extends, stresses, bends.

Ten secs per stretch! she tweet-tweets.

Drew detests her self-betterment.
He swerves the cheerless speech,
tells her the new Merc's very speedy.
She clenches her teeth,
eggy, yet reserved.

Then plebs enter The Ten Bells:
Beth gets tetchy.

Beth's meek. She's never met plebs.
She's never met rebels, sheepbreeders, serfs.
Jeez, Beth's never even seen Bez.

The wretched DJ peddles the cheesy dregs the plebs respect;
the beery lechers get wrecked, then enter senselessness.
They explete freely, they spew phlegm
they sneeze, less Kleenex.

Beth eyes them —
greedy geezers, Ellen Degeneres femmes.
Her cheer depletes keenly.
She resents the seedy jerks, the sexy chests,
Drew's mettle's tested.

See, Beth's never felt seedy,
Beth's never felt greedy,
Beth prefers her sphere teeny-weeny,

her Eden serpent free.

The plebs spy Beth's repelled leer;
they send her the V.
Heckled, The Meek jet.
Stepney's been sleeted.
Drew bleep-bleeps the Merc.

About a Minute

In the time it took you
to tell me what I already knew
a Tesco checkout till went on the blink
some Year Seven students launched a balloon rocket
Joe made a sale
a note was passed in class that read:
Kev Medcraft blows goats
a taxi pulled over for an ambulance
on the Goldhurst Road
John 'ignored' three friend requests
from men he used to play football with
287 people died
patties were flipped
a white paper was launched
Molly burned her hand on the grill
Sky+ boxes were set
Beamers bleeped, doors clicked shut
spoons heated, purses nicked
millions were lost on the stock exchange
P45s were issued
Miranda rang her mum to say she got the job
barrels were changed

coffee burned on drip plates
parliamentary expenses recorded
fathers cried openly in maternity wards
knees were scraped
a jury was dismissed
and in every corner of every town
other hearts were breaking
being pulled in two
by a hushed litany of apologies.

The Ballad of Chris & Ann's Fish Bar

If pictures speak a thousand words
then how about this one?
A chip shop's plastic neon sign
with some of the letters gone.

From a distance it says *Chris Fish Bar*
but then, when you get closer,
filth around the missing letters reveals
that it's supposed to

say *& Ann's. Chris & Ann's Fish Bar.*
One doubts coincidence.
A name removed so neatly
couldn't be an accident.

No, surely just a balding man
with ladder, hammer, chisel,
all mid-life paunch and swallowed tears,
perhaps some grey-skied drizzle.

English has some tragic phrases:
pregnant widow; HIV;
Half Price Boneless Banquet For One;
but this sign did it for me.

~

At the fag end of the eighties,
a food tech NVQ
in a class of seventeen year-olds,
she floated into view.

Her hair a raven spiral perm,
high-waisted, tapered slacks,
banana clips and tons of zips,
her tongue as sharp as tacks.

And Chris, poor lad, just sat and gawped;
he tuned out of the lesson
(and to this day he still can't make
a decent salad dressing).

He'd seen it at the cinema,
a thousand hammy scenes;
he knew the spotty kid could win
the woman of his dreams.

So like his dad did years before
he approached her after class,
stumbled, though not excessively,
then went ahead and asked:

Did she perhaps like watching films?
Did she want to go with him?
A mate worked at the Odeon;
he could maybe sneak them in.

And Ann looked at her lanky suitor,
so desperate to impress,
and though she'd not intended to
her lips just answered: *Yes.*

Chris wasn't like the other lads.
He wasn't like her friends.
He dreamed beyond the terraces
and lagered-up weekends.

For him the NVQ they did
wasn't just a doss.
It was the first time Ann had met
a bloke who gave a toss.

Her father, step-dad, boyfriends hadn't.
Now she looked at Chris —
corduroys and kind eyes — and thought,
Well, I could live with this.

Sure, they went through all the motions:
an escalation of dates,
two fidgety 'meet the parents' meals,
the gradual loss of mates.

But she knew on that first evening
that he satisfied her needs,
that the Odeon and corduroys
would inevitably lead

to a fairly modest civil service
— no hint of wedding list —
reception in the Jurnet Suite
at which their friends got pissed.

And so it did and life rolled on,
left college, settled down,
and when he'd worked five years in kitchens
Chris took a trip to town,

dressed in his pinstriped Burton's suit,
to get himself a loan
to buy a Newtown chip shop,
complete with family home.

Then soon that fated plastic sign
and 'taters everywhere,
with rolled up sleeves and jars of eggs
and chip fat in their hair.

Occasionally a photo op
for the local press:
They're Frying High at this New Plaice;
The Newtown Star's Impressed.

He'd banter with the customers
as she dipped cod in batter
and though their profits were quite slim
it didn't really matter.

His dream was now reality —
everything in place — although
at night he still made little jokes
about spawning their own roe.

And she would laugh and say *Not yet*
and pop her tiny pills —
Come on dear for now at least
let's just pay off some bills.

But something in the way she said it,
perhaps a lack of need,
brushed scales from their relationship;
in time it came to bleed.

For in all this talk of plans and dreams,
of building life while loving,
Chris had contributed everything
and she precisely nothing.

Poor Ann had never dreamed of this,
she'd never really planned;
as passive as the cod she dipped —
a foil to her man.

And as they lived their deep fried life
behind that plastic front
she realised he wasn't what she wanted,
just not what she didn't want.

And of course Chris knew, as we all know
how love can turn and cut you;
rigid in a double bed
in case they try to touch you.

Your backs to one another,
taking turns to cry,
as all your rituals, jokes and glances
flap fruitlessly, then die.

The problem battered, fried, fished out,
they left it in the tray
until the salmonella bred,
until one Saturday

when Chris was shutting up the shop
and couldn't find his keys.
He shouted out into the back:
Ann, I need you please.

He turned to see her standing there,
a parody of a bride,
with lipstick and a fur coat on,
a suitcase at each side.

The freeze frame before the drum roll,
a death knell for old lovers,
a made-for-telly movie scene,
a TV Quick front cover.

The drab cliché turned his stomach.
He sunk into his shoes
as soggy as the chips he sold
wrapped up in last week's news.

How long had he been listening to
the car alarm in bed?
How long had he been pickling
those voices in his head?

How long had he been filleting
the demons at his gate?
She went to pick her cases up,
he found his tongue, said: *Wait.*

That night a storm rolled down Old Street
and put them out to sea;
that night a frost swept through the shop
that froze the mushy peas.

That night they screamed and shook and wept
together on their knees;
a fraught de-boning of their love
with dogged expertise.

He grimly gripped his fishing net,
she wriggled to be free
till in the madness of the sunrise
came his epiphany.

He'd battled all his life uphill
with gritted stoney gumption,
his eyes shut tight with exertion,
hauling an assumption,

and not the load he'd meant to take,
the parcel that was real,
their dust had never settled down;
it was blown about by zeal.

A quick, sick realisation rose.
I built all this for you,
I know, she said, *but that's just it:*
I never asked you to.

But what then, Ann? What do you want?
What is all this about?
She looked at his kind eyes and said:
just let me work that out.

Who knows what I'll discover, Chris.
She took him by the hand.
The room was briefly silent then
he said, *I understand.*

You've got some catching up to do,
the only question's whether
you feel that catching up is something
we can do together.

So, in the morning's shipwrecked sun,
without a hint of drizzle,
he went outside to do the deed:
the ladder, hammer, chisel.

But as her name was chipped away
his wife remained at home
with dreams she never knew she had,
their authorship her own.

See, pictures speak a thousand words,
but many tales are longer,
and love can rot your heart to pulp,
but some loves are stronger.

It's Splendid Being the Infidel

A song for a musical

They say the world is heading for a meltdown.
They tell me change is coming and it must.
They say that we're not free
but if you're asking me
I'd say that most of us aren't all that fussed.

Yes, life is rather jolly here in Britain.
We're lolling in a warm, suggestive fog.
What need of I for vicars
when I can drop my knickers
and write something offensive on my blog?

It's stunning what the human mind can do
unshackled from the fiery threat of hell —
I'm lost in dirty thoughts
and not the least distraught.
Yes, it's splendid being the In-fid-el.

It's wonderful to be the Infidel.
No curate keeping track of all my sins.
When a finger points at me,
it means I've won the lottery:
It's You! Now spend it all on pointless things!

So toss your holy books onto the fire
and come and have a cheeky smoke round mine.
I'm lying in my filth
and perving on G-GILFs —
but panic not, she's only thirty-nine!

I'm bloody thrilled to be the Infidel.
No omnipresent git to cramp my cool.
For life is non-stop gaiety
when you are your own deity,
and you and *only you* can make the rules.

These sad religious wars
are nothing but a bore,
so tell me now how many have been felled?
You'd burn far fewer flags
if you had porno mags.
What price a wank in these Jihadi cells?

Yes, I'd rather be a heathen;
I like my bosoms heaving.
In karma terms I think I do quite well.
And though you find me wanton,
you will never find me wanting.
Oh it's splendid being the In-fi-del.

Houses that Used to Be Boozers

This town has a stark share
of repossessed dark lairs,
of houses that used to be boozers.
Where once we were drinking
we're now slowly sinking
in sofas the colour of bruises.

Ex-sawdust saloons
are now minimalist rooms
where every night somebody chooses
to rest their behind
and half-silence their mind
in a slow death of sweaty-necked snoozes,
in a tap-drip of box sets and docs.

But these houses they used to be buzzing
they used be busting and splitting and spitting and ripe.
These places, they used to be tasteless,
they used to be graceless and legless and feckless each night!

Down lop-sided streets
factory workers would meet
in these houses that used to be boozers.
They'd wash the week's slog
in the honey-dew grog
in their bawdy and dubious rouses.

Now ladies frizz hair
in the Glade Plug-in air
of these houses that used to be boozers.
So far from the funk
of the blood, sweat and spunk
when these houses were floozy-filled boozers.
When these houses were ringing with song.

And I long for the throng of the song when we thrived
in these dives with their ligging and frigging and dirt.
These hell-holes where black-hearted arseholes
would pour souls, then sing and kick heads in till everything hurt.

Farewell Rose & Crown
for The Ship has gone down,
and she's no more for rum-infused cruises.
The mad Horse & Dray
is not braying today
he's muzzled as McIntyre muses.

The clatters of pewter
now taps on computers
in houses that used to be boozers.
Hum-drum sobriety —
there's no society —
houses that used to be boozers.

In cordoned-off hush
we are turning to mush
in these houses that used to be boozers,

we're fingering phones
and we're drinking alone
in these houses that used to be boozers.

A Shed of One's Own

All that he asks is that now and again
we will leave him alone to tinker with metals
or squint at the telly. I've plagued him for decades
with know-it-all banter and insolent whimsy
just after a rise to remind me he loves me.

I'm modern and I wear my heart on my feed,
my thoughts on display for the tourists to see.
Describing emotions comes naturally
and at time I have thought him sardonic and surly.
I've picked at his bones with my lazy degree.

But now, with my afternoons measured in nappies
and Rubik's Cube schedules that tally so rarely
I'm starting to see life from over his shoulder.
Our sighs harmonise as we fix on our targets:
some peace in the evenings, a shed of one's own.